AF481153

AFRICAN-AMERICANS WHO FOUGHT IN THE AMERICAN REVOLUTION

History of the United States
Children's History Books

In this book, we're going to talk about African-Americans during the American Revolution. So, let's get right to it!

Storming Fort Wagner

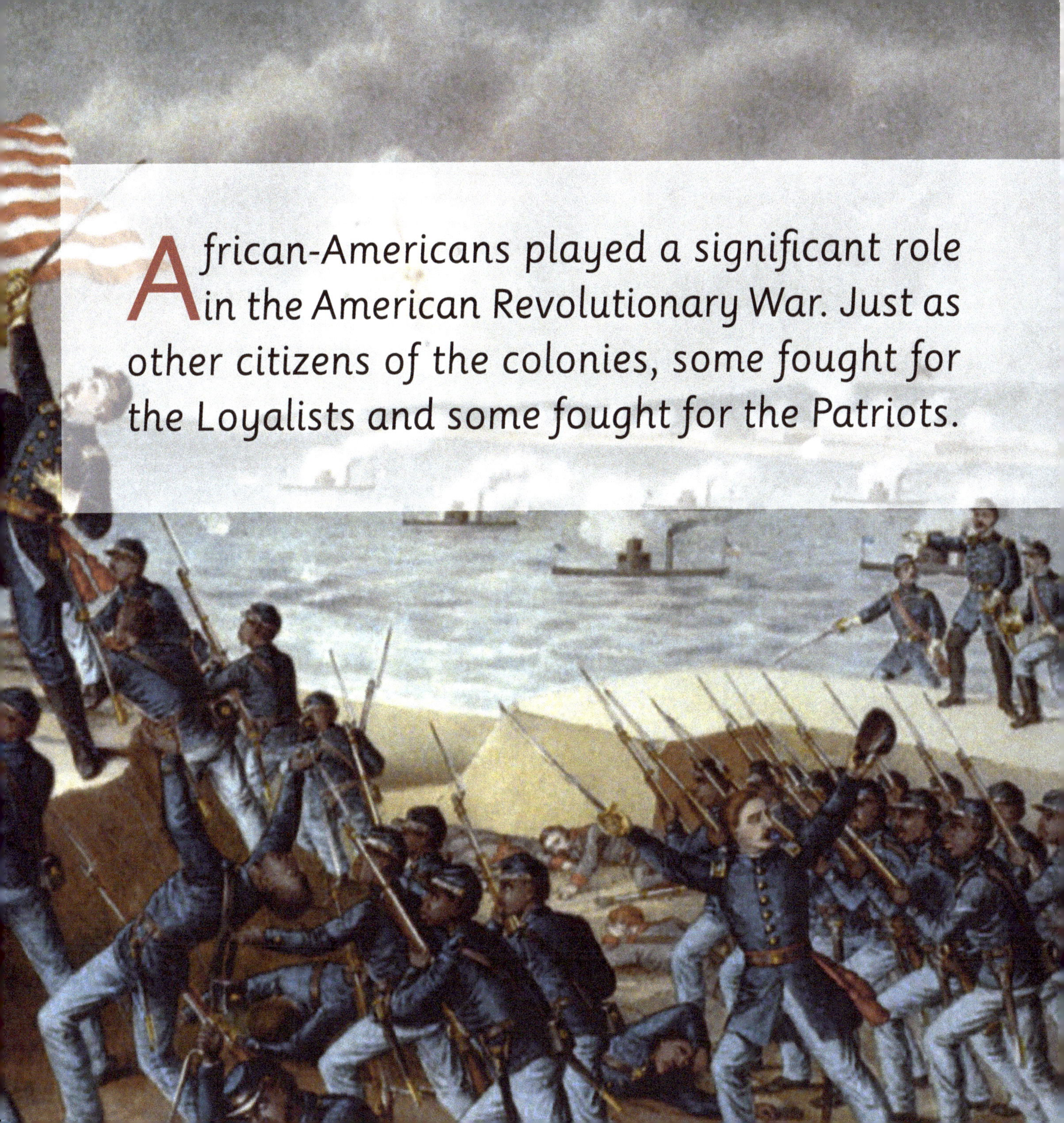

African-Americans played a significant role in the American Revolutionary War. Just as other citizens of the colonies, some fought for the Loyalists and some fought for the Patriots.

There were many reasons that African-Americans participated in the Revolutionary War. Some men made a choice to enlist. Others were forced to because they were slaves. Here are some of the reasons:

* They wanted to be free. They had been promised freedom after the war. Both the Loyalists and Patriots had made this promise.
* They wanted adventure.

Defeat of the Ashantees

U.S. MAIL

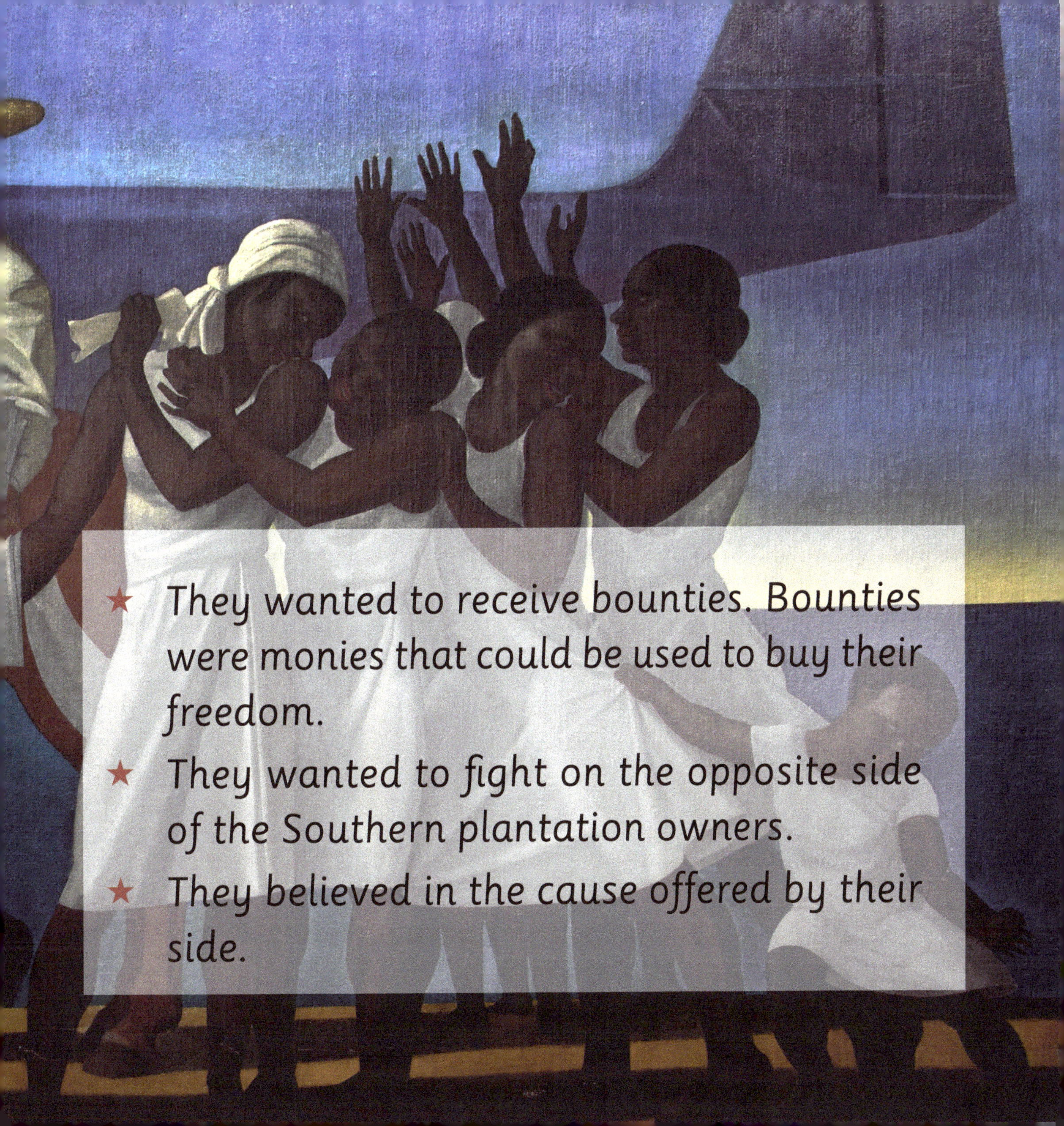

- ★ They wanted to receive bounties. Bounties were monies that could be used to buy their freedom.
- ★ They wanted to fight on the opposite side of the Southern plantation owners.
- ★ They believed in the cause offered by their side.

HOW MANY AFRICAN-AMERICANS WERE LIVING IN THE COLONIES?

About one-fifth of the population in the colonies was made up of citizens of African descent. The majority of African-Americans were slaves, but this didn't prevent them from fighting as soldiers and patriots. Some participated in spy missions as well.

African American slaves

The very first person killed as part of the fight for American independence was an African-American runaway slave by the name of Crispus Attucks. In 1770, tensions between the British soldiers and colonists were at an all-time high due to the heavy taxes the British were levying on the colonists.

The Boston Massacre

Crispus Attucks

A British officer who was unable to house his soldiers in a suitable building had them pitch tents in the public square in Boston. The soldiers and colonists began to get into a brawl.

It's not clear, but some historians believe that Crispus was leading a group of Patriots to confront the British and made the first move by wielding a stick. Others say that he was standing there leaning on the stick. In any case, Crispus put himself in harm's way for the cause. The British opened fire and Crispus along with several others was killed.

The Patriots

PATRIOTS OR LOYALISTS?

The African-American population in the colonies had split loyalties. Some were loyal to the parent country. Others wanted America to be independent. Most of all, those who were slaves wanted their own freedom.

Early in the conflict, the British openly invited slaves and indentured servants to join their army. They promised freedom to those who fought with them and many African-Americans decided that this was the right choice for them.

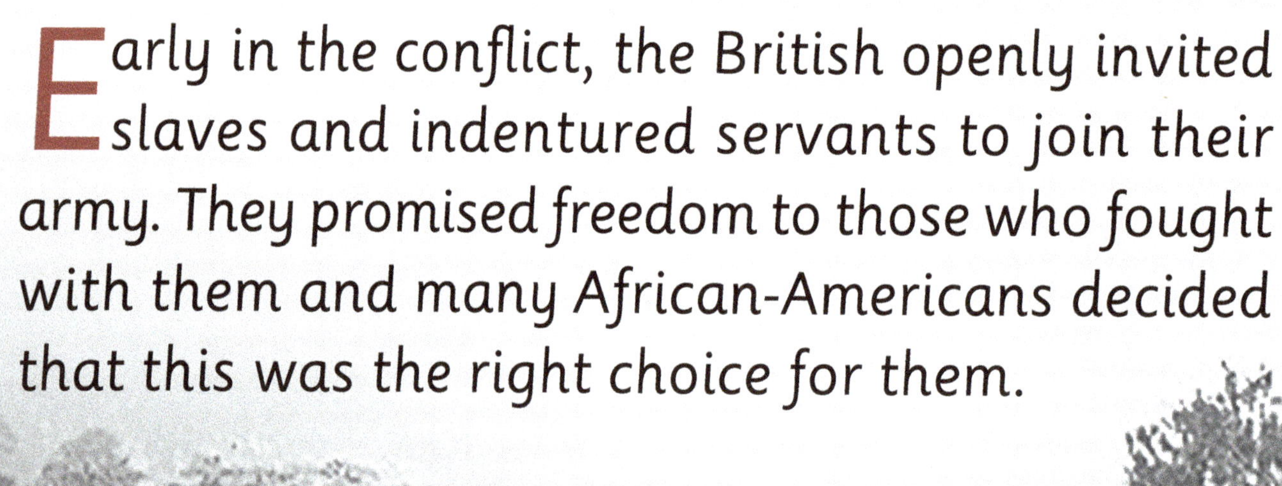

Black American Slaves

The Continental Army, the army of the colonists, didn't accept African-American soldiers until 1775 and at the beginning they only accepted free men. Slaves were enlisted beginning in 1776. They were promised that they would be given freedom when the war was over. Despite the slower start with the Continental Army, most African-Americans joined the Patriots as opposed to the Loyalists.

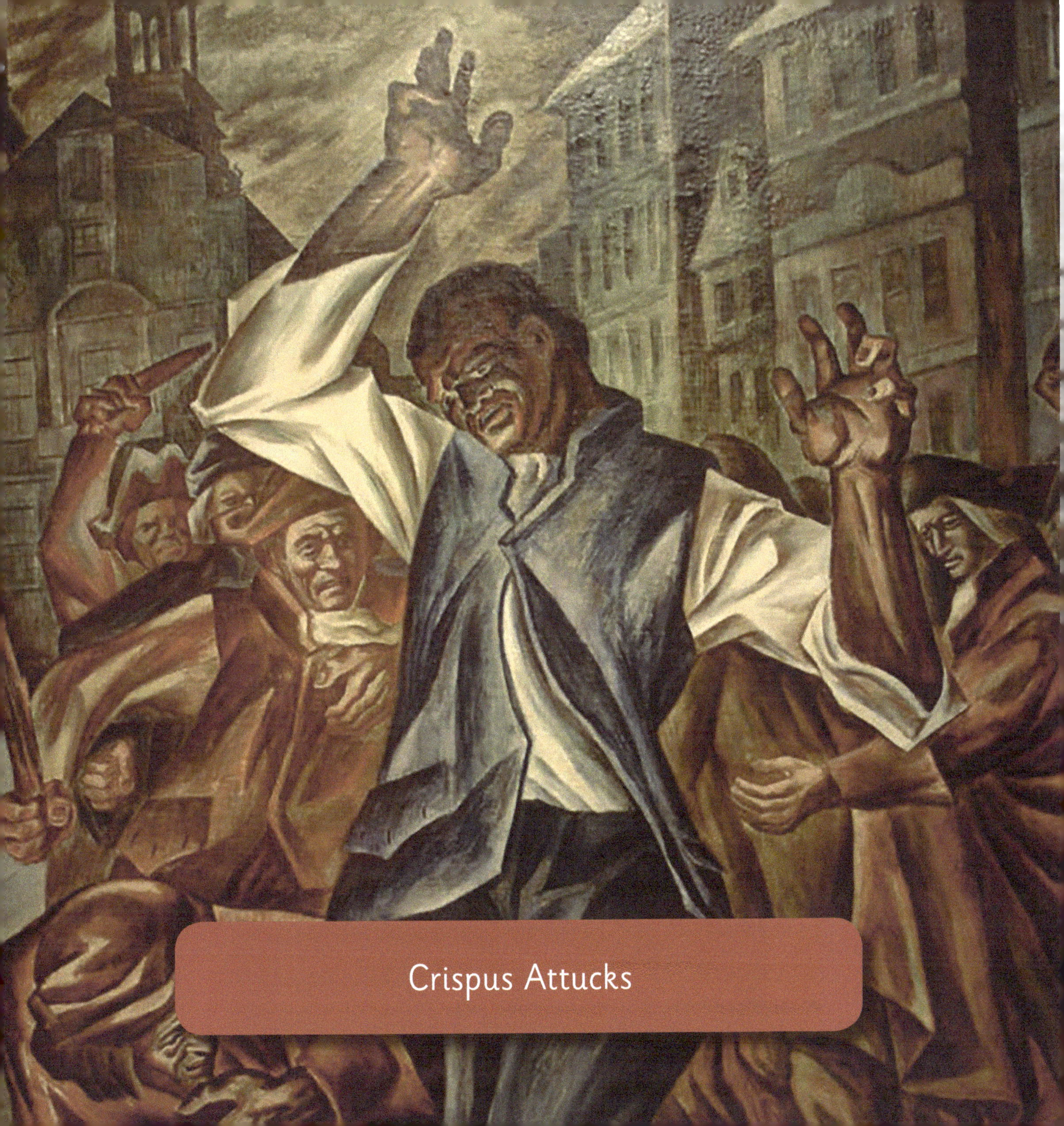

Crispus Attucks

American soldiers

There were approximately 9,000 African-American soldiers. They joined the Continental Army as well as the Navy. Some were soldiers in the state militia. Others were Army wagoneers, which simply means they were responsible for the wagons and supplies. Many were servants who worked for officers in the Army or Navy.

THE REVOLUTIONARY WAR BEGINS

Prior to the Revolution, some African-Americans had become Minutemen. These soldiers got the name "Minutemen" because they were trained to be ready for battle within a minute's notice. Some African-Americans served in private armies as Minutemen to defend their villages against Native Americans.

American Revolutionary War

Salem Poor

By 1775, the Congress had given orders to the Massachusetts military that they should be ready at a minute's notice if the British struck the first blow in Boston. Peter Salem, a slave who had been freed by his master, was part of the Minutemen militia in Framingham, Massachusetts.

Once the war started, he enlisted and served for over five years. After the war, Salem was able to keep his freedom. However, many slaves who had been promised freedom were denied that freedom by their masters once the war was over. The Patriots had fought for a free country but African-Americans weren't given those same rights, even though they had fought for them.

Peter Salem shoots Major Pitcairn at Bunker Hill

At the Battles of Lexington and Concord in the spring of 1775, many African-Americans fought on the Patriot side. Prince Estabrook, who had been a slave and was a Minuteman, was wounded during the battle. The critical Battle of Bunker Hill had African-American Patriots and white Patriots fighting side by side.

During the battle, Peter Salem killed John Pitcairn, who was a British commander.

*S*ome of the African-American names that remain from that history are:

- ➲ **Peter Salem,** a former slave and Minute-man who enlisted
- ➲ **Salem Poor,** a former slave who enlisted and became a war hero
- ➲ **Barzillai Lew,** a former servant who became a distinguished soldier

African-American soldiers
World War II

Soldiers of World War II

- **Blaney Grusha,** a former servant
- **Titus Coburn,** a former slave
- **Alexander Ames,** a former slave
- **Cato Howe,** possibly a free man before he enlisted
- **Seymour Burr,** originally joined the British but was returned to his owner and then joined the Continental Army

JOINING THE PATRIOTS

African-Americans were motivated to join the Patriots because they thought they would win their freedom. They assumed that in risking their lives and gaining their freedom that they would forever change the injustice toward African-Americans.

They had assumed that their civil rights would be equivalent to the rights given to whites in the new country. During the war, they participated as soldiers as well as messengers. They also served as guides and some were recruited as spies.

As new troops were needed for the Continental Armed Forces, the regiments in New England persuaded African-American slaves to enlist with the promise of freedom if they survived the war. Around 1781, the army's troops were about 25% African-Americans.

AFRICAN-AMERICAN SAILORS

The shortage of manpower at sea was a serious problem during the Revolutionary War. Both the British Royal Navy and the Continental Navy enlisted sailors who were African-Americans.

African-American Sailor

Courageous Act of Cyrus Tiffany in Battle of Lake Erie

Even the colonies in the south, who feared the prospect of slaves being armed with guns, didn't seem to have any issues with them piloting ships or shooting cannons. Some state navies, such as the navy of South Carolina, had a large number of African-Americans piloting their ships. Sometimes Patriots captured African-Americans from the British Royal Navy and had them pilot the Continental Navy's ships.

Both the leaders of the Revolution and the British leaders were fearful of African-Americans turning upon them now that they were armed. Slave owners were concerned that they might be harmed. They felt that handing African-Americans this power would mean that the southern way of life with slaves who did the master's bidding would be over as a result.

Inspection and sale of a slave

African American Slaves

The British were concerned about a rebellion being started by slaves during the war. They knew that southern plantation owners didn't want their slaves in possession of guns. For a while, the British only used African-Americans as skilled workers and spies instead of soldiers in the South.

THE FATE OF AFRICAN-AMERICAN LOYALISTS

As the Revolutionary War was winding down, it was clear that African-Americans and other Loyalists would need to flee the country. During the evacuation of Charleston in South Carolina in 1782, about 5,000 African-Americans with many Loyalists left for resettlement in Jamaica and the West Indies. Here the Loyalists started plantations with slave labor. About half of these African-Americans were Loyalists' slaves.

First black Senator and Representatives

Slaves who had been promised freedom in exchange for fighting on the British side, crowded into New York City awaiting their fate. The British created a registry and issued

certificates to those who would be given their freedom and transported to Nova Scotia in Canada.

THE FATE OF AFRICAN-AMERICAN PATRIOTS

In the twenty years after the Revolution was over, many slaves were given their freedom. By 1810, the number of African-Americans who were free had reached over 185,000, about 13 percent of their overall population. Many of the states in the North created laws against slavery, but as time progressed slavery became more entrenched in the South due to the need for labor on plantations.

Creole woman with her slave

African-American families celebrate the home-coming of the 369th Army infantry unit.

In most cases, both African-American soldiers and white soldiers lived and fought side by side during the American Revolution. There was one regiment that was known as an African-American regiment because most of the soldiers were African-American or mixed race. That regiment was called the 1st Rhode Island Regiment and was also known as Varnum's Continentals.

AFTER THE WAR WAS OVER

Many of the African-American men who risked their lives during the war were granted their freedom. However, the freedom afforded them was not the same as the freedom offered to white men. There's a difference between not being a slave and being truly free to all available opportunities.

White and black working together

United States Capitol

Despite the fact that African-Americans had fought for America's freedoms, the United States Congress enacted a law in 1792 that prevented them from enlisting in the military. It took until the 1960s for there to be some movement toward total equality for African-Americans.

Frederick Douglass
Harriet Tubman
Alexander T. Augusta
Martin Luther King

Awesome! Now you know more about the achievements of African-Americans during the American Revolution. You can find more History books from Baby Professor by searching the website of your favorite book retailer.

Visit

BABY PROFESSOR
EDUCATION KIDS

www.BabyProfessorBooks.com

to download Free Baby Professor eBooks
and view our catalog of new and exciting
Children's Books